T0006084

"A tender yet visceral collection that spoke to my big bisexual heart. Weissmann's words find the romance in the everyday, transporting us through formative moments of a life well loved."

— JEN WINSTON
author of *Greedy*

"*Her, Him & I* is sensual, wistful, and earnest. This collection gorgeously balances the dualities of hope and heartbreak, nostalgia and anticipation, flirtation and loathing, playfulness and sincerity. Your heart will ache in your chest as Christian illustrates what it means to move on, defy, and bloom."

— MADISEN KUHN
author of *Almost Home*

"From the very first line, Weissmann builds a vulnerable world of love, lust, and loss. You will feel with him, you will yearn with him, you will sigh in relief, and ultimately you will hope with him. Weissmann has proved themselves as a young poet to look out for through their debut collection, which illuminates the importance of falling for oneself."

— ELI RALLO
author of *I Didn't Know I Needed This*

"Weissmann has choreographed a dance with words— beautifully capturing how the relationships of our youth teach us things about ourselves we'd never learn otherwise."

— MICHAELA ANGEMEER
author of *Please Love Me at My Worst*

"Weissmann's *Her, Him & I* is a necessary addition to the queer literary canon. It is a collection of poems that gives, to its readers, permission: to feel, to pine after whomever."

— GRANT CHEMIDLIN
author of *What We Lost in the Swamp*

"Christian makes poetry feel so fresh and modern. His words remind us that love is the most important thing, the only thing, really."

— RENE LYNCH
editor at *LAist* & *LA Times*

Her, Him & I

poems

Christian Weissmann

central avenue
POETRY

2024

For the Qs

Copyright © 2024 Christian Weissmann
Cover and internal design © 2024 Central Avenue Marketing Ltd.
Illustrations: iStock @derno & @shironosov; CreativeMarket @undrey

All rights reserved. No part of this book may be used or reproduced in any manner
whatsoever without written permission from the author except in the case of brief
quotations embodied in critical articles and reviews.

This is a work of fiction. Names, characters, places and incidents either are the
product of the author's imagination or are used fictitiously and any resemblance to
actual persons, living or dead, business establishments, events or locales is entirely
coincidental.

Published by Central Avenue Poetry
an imprint of Central Avenue Marketing Ltd.
centralavenuepublishing.com
@centavepoetry

HER HIM & I

Trade Paperback: 978-1-77168-373-9
EPUB: 978-1-77168-374-6

Published in Canada
Printed in United States of America

1. POETRY / LGBT   2. POETRY / Subjects & Themes - Love

1 3 5 7 9 10 8 6 4 2

"I KNEW WHO I WAS THIS MORNING,
BUT I'VE CHANGED A FEW TIMES SINCE THEN."

—LEWIS CARROLL

Dear Reader,

This is a journey through my overthinking mind.

It is a road map for chasing individuality. Racing after other people
to find it. Begging for someone else to eradicate the emptiness I carry.
Peeking into the eyes of men and women, substance and scripture,
hoping that I'll catch a glimpse of who I'm supposed to be. Dancing in
every catastrophe, praying I'll find something real.

This is a book centered around the romantic relationships in my life.
While there is not a singular "her" or "him," each pronoun is meant to
represent a love affair of mine.

Throughout this story, I'm figuring out how and where to land on
the ever-tipping scale of sexuality. I'm trying to leave the bounds of a
binary label behind me. I'm attempting to rewire my psyche, in hopes
of giving myself the answers I need.

(Spoiler alert: I don't have all of them yet. But I'm learning.)

Come to these pages and find solace. Let each poem be an example of
how to conciliate the human condition—particularly the experience of
being queer and devastatingly lovesick.

There is joy here. There is loss. But ultimately, there is hope.

X

— Christian

I

BEHAVING IN A CROWD

JET LAG

It's two a.m. in the East Village.
You're frolicking up Fifth Street
with my red string tied around your wrist,
breathing in the changing seasons,
anticipating and dreaming of the endless future.

It's eleven p.m. in Silver Lake.
I'm walking down West Sunset Boulevard
with your white ring wrapped around my fourth finger,
inhaling the secondhand smoke,
reminiscing and rethinking every single part of our past.

SHADES OF RED

His auburn hair and hazel eyes
glimmer across the Hudson River.
As you lock your left hand onto his right,
the butterflies flow through your veins.
The two of you
sit there
intertwined,

as this heartbreak
shakes my palms
and bleeds through
every vessel in my body.

SNOOZE

The alarm clock
burns my eardrums,
gallivanting into my thoughts
at this ungodly hour,
jumping up and down on my nightstand
like a three-year-old
wanting Mommy's attention.

Well, I don't reward
temper tantrums!

The alarm clock is broken.

SAN FERNANDO SUNDAY

The birds here chirp at noon
and I can't remember your favorite color anymore.

You always woke up with the sun.

The mocha pot was finished
by the time I made it to the kitchen.
Water in a coffee mug, it is.

Maybe it was red.

THE FOOL

Over the past few years,
I've cried hundreds of tears,
counted thousands of regrets
and longed for a love
that millions want
but few ever achieve.
Looking for permanent fulfillment
in temporary lovers,
tarot card videos
and empty whiskey bottles.
The search for extrinsic meaning
is a journey I set sail on years ago
and I'm scared to jump ship.

KING MUIR ROAD

On warmer evenings,
I open up the porch screen
and leave the vinyl running
just to hear the static sing.

I'm a child again,
sitting in front of a raging bonfire,
alone and filled with peace!

I often miss those days.
It was a tranquil life of

        turning the other way,

making a choice

        to ignore the horrors that went on
        behind those bedroom doors

and singing myself to sleep.

7 LB. 8 OZ.

Born into a February hailstorm,
carried into the arms of
the song who will
soon forget my name.

They spit addiction
onto each piano key,
demanding I drink their emission
like a posthumous inheritance.

I call for a doctor
because they refuse to sing for a sponsor.

"It's no use trying to fix the tempo, simply join the dance!"

I sway back and forth
as I forge my bets of "changing the cycle"
into their best bottle of whiskey.

When I come up for air,
I'm sent to the front lawn
with the rest of the dreamers
to patch up paint on their white picket fence.

I chew on their loose tobacco
as the sky begins to cry onto my cheeks.

I wipe my face
as their melody sneaks into my eardrums yet again, stating,
"Hey! You missed a spot."

JOURNAL ENTRY #12

There are so many things I'm forbidden to share,
but I'll say them anyway.

I'm eleven years old,
almost twelve!

I'm sitting on my twin-sized bed,
while the cicadas sing a steady hymn
outside my bedroom window.

The sun overstays its welcome this time of year.
I watch through dusted shutters as she finally lays herself to rest.

I can smell the charcoal from my father's bonfire, down in the poppy
field.

Arrowheads are outside, waiting to be carved.
But they'll have to wait.
Wait for me to make something of myself.

Do you ever wonder where you'll be in ten years?

I know where I'll be.
A movie star
living in California,
a place to call my own,
with a ~~girl,~~ boy, someone to make me laugh.

After I'm done here,
I'll hide these wishes in the attic

and carve out every step myself.

Hoping that one day,
I can finally look in the mirror
and see an honest person.

BEIGE OR BURGUNDY?

The cashmere vibrations
fill my body with temporary comfort.
She hugs me seductively
and whispers salacious secrets in my ear.
She tucks me into bed
and creaks my mouth open for air,
leaving me ready
to breathe open a new day,
pining after her all over again.

I've never kept a bottle of wine more than a week.

FERN DELL DRIVE

The pine tree
next to the west branch
of Griffith Observatory
dances quietly
on Sunday afternoons,
conscious of the storm to come
but trying to move in the moment,
half-naked enjoyment.

I am a tree,
trepidation dancing in the wind!

When will I be able to
recognize the fear,
sit with it
and choose to love myself anyways?

BEST BY SEPT. 27

Every evening absent of her
waters down the moments of misery
I can barely seem to recall.
Now all I can remember
is the taste of expired blueberries on my tongue
and a burnt coffee kettle on my knuckles.

My esteemed loneliness washes away
the anguish of our chilled cataclysm
leaving my mind as
a blank canvas of   dissociation
except for an imperfect black dot
burgeoning   dead center
ruining the virgin material.
That little speck of immortality
is colored in the vein of   my faults,
                                my shortcomings,
                                my insecurity.

You were the landscape of possibility
and I was the wretched blemish on your future.

LIQUID LOBOTOMY

I crave emotional peace,
yet I'm addicted
to feasting upon memories of the past
that leave stab wounds in my lower back.
My nervous system is devoted
to a life of neurosis.
Uncertainty is my cocktail of choice
and it's about time
I put the drink down.

SATIN

I've avoided your side of the bed
for the last fourteen days.

Until this evening,
I caught myself
searching for the evidence
of your heartbeat
on the wrinkled pillowcase.

Some little limerick of you
to corroborate
that you once loved me long enough
to linger in my linen.

I wish I could say
I've forgotten you
just like I should,
but I'm still looking
for the memory of you
within these disheveled sheets.

MAY FLOWERS

You got offered a rebirth
the second you walked out my door.
Yet, here I am!
Trapped in my past life,
pacing around the hospital bed,
waiting for each minute to pass by
so I, too,
can be transcended.

I'll call it my situation of crisis.
The old me is still dying,
but the new me
has not been born yet.

PLAYING CHECKERS

She dances on a sweaty bar tile
as the rose beams seep through
the projection screen.
Am I projecting?
Or do you feel this too?
What I'm trying to say is...
Are you open to feeling what this could be?
Not shoes clacking on a checkered floor,
but our feet dancing under the crimson sheets
as my lips graze your collarbone.

Collar Bone
Bone what?

Oh no,
I'm too nervous
to do that so soon!
See, I need time
to see your soul spin
before I can let my heartbeat
into your quilted palms.
But for now,
let's allow the beat of the song
and the pit pit patter
of our checkerboard shoes
to give us a taste of what
the music of us
could feel like
once we reach the chorus.
Actually, let's listen now.

S. BROADWAY AVE.

Her skin synced up to mine,
singing lustful notes of harmony
as the crimson red glow of string lights
faded onto her torso
and reflected into my soul.

I looked deep into those Bambi eyes
and saw her universe
opening right up
just for me.

CRUSH

I sit on the memory of summer
until my legs blister,
sucker punched,
hoping I gain the courage
to call you up
and make you feel inferior;
revealing the oddity that
someone made love to me
once you were no longer around.

TADALAFIL?

Moments of intimacy
sit on a malfunctioning pendulum
of nirvana and lost art for me.

A moment of presence and pleasure
can completely consume me
just for it to be stomped on
by tremors of the past.

I breathe a sigh of relief when we're done!

Not because I finished,
but because I gave my anxiety some hell today.
Why can't it ever be black and white?
Every good day seems to be followed by
a weekend of disconnection.
When will I rid myself of the thoughts
that keep me from becoming the man
I told her I could be?

999

Lipstick stain on the television screen,
blistering moments of passion
now dancing in the not-so-distant

Past

I clocked my cigarette like a revolver
and let the gunpowder spew onto my overflowing ashtray,
trying to stop the game of hopscotch that

Fear

was playing in my head
and fought to find peace
in her heavy eyes that were quickly growing

Dull

like the questions of tomorrow
humming through the AC unit:
are we still

Us?

OLIVE OIL

Mixing oil and vinegar
on your bedside table,
staining the painted wood
with shades of the present moment.

Hoping ocean eyes
can carry us through
the white of the storm ahead.

We keep running back
to the sensation of our first night.
Your dress ripped and
my trousers torn.
The smell of strawberries filled my nose
as we were catching stars with our tongues.

But when the clouds creep back into our periphery
all we have left is acid on your nightstand.

Yes,
some stains might stay
and some will fade,
but the only everlasting mark
is our memory.

Just like the tight grip of her hand
when I whispered,
"I just want to make you happy."

NO. 5

I recall the sweetest love of yesterday
when I smell a perfume
that sings notes like yours
or fall into a stranger's bed
that I can sink my weight of the day into
just like I did yours.

When did those sheets become ice-cold?
When did the smell of orchids
begin to diminish
into a charcoal aroma of melancholy
seeping onto every relic of you?

MORNING ROUTINE

My day-to-day
is an overly accentuated stretch of the truth
just so I can fill my
oh so fragile
ego with temporary stability.

Why can't I be content
with the reality of my circumstances?
I seem to live by the phrase,
"Fake it till you make it!"
But I seem to be exhausting all avenues of *faking it,*
without making any ends come to a head.

Some say that suffering is the glue
that holds humanity together,
yet I am constantly falling apart.

When will the last shoe drop?

MASOCHIST BOTANIST

I live on the busy street corners,
in reverberant cafes
and in the crowded kitchens of a Friday night party.
Find me at any affair that keeps me
from growing comfortable enough
to confess my sinful truths to another naked eye.

I've been accustomed to
concealing the lavender bud
that lives under my symmetrical sleeves.
But as each Friday passes,
the flower is getting stronger.
Blooming leaves of immorality
from the bend of my arm
to the edges of my worn-out wrists.
Ripening my palms with purple pollen
that gets tougher to wash off
every time I turn on the sink.

But if I pack on the layers,
keep the mirrors covered with cotton towels
and refrain from any fifty-minute session on a chaise longue,
I'll be safe for a while longer.

If I play the game
and refrain from my own song and dance,
I can be a mere whisper in the breeze.

Unseen, unfelt, like a secret among the trees.

C-SHARP

Tell me everything your mind asks you not to.

Use me like a racket you can bounce
every thought,   every fear,
            every joke,   every whisper,
every sweat,
        every tear,
                right off of.

                I want to be your sounding board in this silent town.

Let the noise of bare feet   running down the hallway
            sing to us like a symphony.

Listen to every pillow hit the floor
        as you make a cove for yourself   between my thighs.

Fill my eardrums with your moans of white
trickling
        like blood down my neck.

Let paint splatter along the bedroom walls
telling this space   what the definition of music is.

Cry out to me
    yet again
        and again
            and again

Let me hear you.

In fact,
let me see you

                                       all of you
                 for once.

I promise: nobody will tell.

SWEET SIXTEEN

Is youth truly wasted on the young?

I'm twenty-three years old
and I often find myself chasing after
shadowed memories of my teenage years.
I frequently find myself longing for
the exhilarating ignorance of adolescence,
when there was no ticking timer on self-discovery.

Begging my parents to let me stay out past midnight.
Getting drunk on the icy tiles of Jasper's kitchen.
Taking Alyssa up to Lake Hollywood Park and kissing her on blue
swings.
Lying under a wisdom tree and looking at the iridescent lights of
possibility.
Running around the city like they just declared War Is Over.
Everything tasted new.
Every experience was untrodden ground.

It's a double-edged sword
to recognize how I spent my teen years longing to be older,
and now that I've reached that mountainous "peak"
I pinned in my brain,

I'm ready to reverse time.

LIQUID COURAGE

I spill my heart out to anyone who will listen
to my implicit memory of her.
I repeat the story of where it went wrong
over and over again,
hoping it will rid me of that inner darkness;
yet it never seems to leave.
I just end up feeling drained of my optimism
with my soul clutching a framed picture of us,
the protective glass smashed down the middle,
with shards taking up whatever is left
of my emotional real estate.

ONE NEW NOTIFICATION

Social scrolling
until my eyes bleed.
I second-guess
every step,
every ex,
every guy,
who is just like me
but better!

How are we meant to find this a tool
when it's shaped like a rake
being stabbed into our self-confidence?

LATE SEPTEMBER

As the leaves fall early this autumn,
I work on trying to forget her.

"A Song for You" plays
through the built-in speakers
of my chestnut vinyl
as I ponder the idea of someone.
Someone else.
Someone different.
Someone new.

I sing to the hope of tomorrow,
praying for the privilege
to understand
the enigma of my heart.

Each lyric drenches my chest
with lilac tears,
painting my present
with a new set of eyes;
unfettered and unbound.

YOUNG HEARTS RUN FREE

When a relationship comes to a close
it's very normal
to feel like you're dying.
A piece of you is,
and a new version of you
is growing in that empty spot.
A scab of succession
is mending over,
the lesson has been learned,
your karmic contract
with that person,
that experience,
that love
is over.

Let go of trying to save the soul
that belonged to yesterday
and welcome the heart
that yearns to run forward.

II

SETTING MYSELF ON FIRE

THE DIVINE SACRAMENT

The first time I kissed a boy
I hid under the chestnut pew of a Catholic church
praying to Mother Mary for a sort of salvation
from the soul that sang inside of me.

The first time I kissed a boy
I took the Eucharist
like it was birthday cake,
hoping to cleanse myself
with the holiest of bodies and blood,
feeling the sprinkles of immorality
dance around in my upset stomach.

The first time I kissed a boy
I cut myself on the metal partition
of the priest's confessional,
scraping my fingers for any sense of sincerity,
hemorrhaging to be seen as a penitent child.

The first time I slept with a boy
I took him to an abandoned church
and swallowed him like he was Communion,
falling in love with his reflection
through the stained-glass windows.

0:00 — 3:51

It was like the room was filled with broken clocks.

Your touch electrified a feeling
that made the hairs on my neck
dance in ubiquitous harmony.

It was you and me.

                                        Then, real life resumed.

But even after the clock intervened,
it was you and me.

ANGEL HAIR

My heart was in Mars
and his lived in Venus.
Our constellation exploded
into a microcosm of stars
every time his fingers matched up with mine.

Get off at Exit 77
and meet me at the Stardust Motel!
Turn off your headlights
and I'll be the aura tonight.

RAVENOUS LOVE

I didn't know the staunch definition
of needing someone
until I looked into the unclouded reflection
and saw a chunk of my beating heart
absent from my chest.

I followed the crimson tracks
and eventually found it residing
near the biting waves
somewhere in a castle off Cleo Street.

I knocked on the door
and there it was.
He held it so gently
and asked if he could keep it
in return for half of his.

I accepted the offer without question
as I knew my heartbeat,
scabs and all,
hadn't sounded so healthy
since he got ahold of it.

TWELVE MONTHS ON THE MOON

I watched his hands
as he cut up an expired credit card
and signed up for a new lease on life.

My neck was drenched in the taste of him
as we slow danced in the guest bathroom,
shedding the weight of our perilous pasts.

I sipped on his mother's merlot
as I watched him draw me from memory.
It was surrealism,
all evening long.

LAVENDER TUESDAYS

Love lies in the in-between.
Sunday mornings
flipping through fiction as I hold his honest hand.
Monday afternoons
sharing a joint in the name of our passion.
Tuesdays at dusk
sketching his structure into my moleskin
soles hanging off the bedside,
feeling like we've got wings in our ankles.

Love is finding contentment
in the small moments.

It's looking into their eyes
and getting lost
in the promise of tomorrow.

LA DAME DE FER

Strolling down the Seine,
declaring our love with a locked key.
I'm planning ahead as you live in the moment,
both fighting to abolish artificial expectations,
falling short
but kissing each other anyway.

The top of the hour
glistened onto our lips.
The aroma of pink peonies
intoxicated the voices in our head saying,
We're running too fast on the cobblestone streets!

We didn't care.
It was right.
We were right.

No auburn song of tears could ruin that now.

LE PETIT PRINCE

J'espère que quand tu regardes par ta fenêtre
et dedans le ciel
tu me vois dans les ètoiles.

I hope when you look out your window
and into the sky
you see me in the stars.

ME AND MY HUSBAND

Long after the sun sets,
I trace the headlights
that paint themselves onto my ceiling.

Shades of ash light up
just to fade in a flash,
seeing which spotlights
make it to the end of my empty walls.

Is this all I have tonight?

Without you here
I count the beams
like a deer lost in his own trance.

One.
One, two, three.
One, two, three, four.
One, two, three, four, five, six.
Six beams.
His lucky number is six, right?

I'd like to say that our relationship is perfectly healthy
but I'm nothing short of flustered
when you're not within reach.

Is this what they call codependency?

COFFEE GROUNDS

I send him pictures of my empty coffee cups
just to hear his daily prophecy.

"Telophase"

Time for growth.
Time to shed leaves of the past
and bloom into new beginnings.
Blossoming for ourselves and for each other.

I feel the string of our love
pull tight across the miles
that stand between us.
Is this a sonnet of growth
or an ode of retribution?

DWINDLING IN OZ

I watch your eyes fawn
at the scuffed-up fork
that lives a stagnant life
on your side of the dinner table.
You avoid my gaze,
grabbing your phone, and get lost in a message
that probably "has nothing to do with me."
I want to ask.
But I know I shouldn't.
I have so many questions
I wouldn't dare to ask the answer to.
Because why would I pay any attention
to the man behind the curtain!
After seven minutes of silence,
you realize *the show must go on!*
One kiss to the right side of my face.
Offering a love language of mine
in compensation
for falling short at another.

Alright, you earned yourself twenty minutes.

Your cheeks bleed a shade of ruby red.
But your lips feel ice-cold.

THE EAST VILLAGE ROCKETTES

One frigid February evening in the village...
Two twenty-something girls
who sipped one too many martinis
sauntered down First Avenue
with one Jimmy Choo on
and another in their purse.

They laughed and they cried
as they danced past each bodega,
eventually stumbling upon
two twenty-something boys
headed home from a dinner date.

They spontaneously grabbed onto the queer strangers,
beseeching for aid on their journey home.

The twenty-something boys quickly obliged,
tossing their arms around each girl   *Rockette style*
safely sashaying their way back to the girls' apartment
as they belted "Teenage Dirtbag" for thirteen blocks.

When they reached the tinted glass of O'Hanlon's
the gals kissed their gays in shining armor goodbye
and went about their merry way.

The boys tangoed on the last few steps of their stroll,
commending themselves on their brief moment
of unbridled intimacy with total strangers,
encapsulating the age-old paradigm
that there still are "good people everywhere."

You just occasionally have to dance with them to find out.

THE SAILOR SONG

Slow dancing to nothing
but the sound of sirens.
Your feet on top of mine,
then mine on yours.

We move in unison,
swinging back and forth,
never-ending
just like the story of us.

THE PATH

Jumping from one yard sale to the next
on a misty Saturday afternoon,
like Tortoise and the Hare,
a regular Frog and Toad.
I take the shortcuts
but my eyes always
find their way back to you
effortlessly enjoying the present
and you never fail to carry me back
to the most extraordinary moments of simplicity.
Our hands write a contract together,
a complex divorce from fearful anticipation,
signing the dotted line, *I must!*

FRANK'S FANTASY

Whiskey rye
Lost in the dreams
Witchcraft
Magic seeps through
and onto

hold the ice
that are close enough to reach
conducting through the jukebox
the sound waves
his fingertips.

HOMEBODY

As I watch you splash tones
on my dining table,
I fold our laundry
mixed together; just like our lives now.
Delicates washed
and hung up in my overflowing closet.
I'll give you the good hangers
because you must know that these walls,
those sheets,
this place
is not home
without you.

PILLOW TALK

Tracing the lines of my tattooed heart,
breathing hopefuls into my anxious chest,
rubbing your leg onto mine.
A single kiss to my waistband
that I'll cherish
long after the indentation fades away,
because you'll still be mine . . .

Right?

SOMETHING IN THE AIR

The pink satin
slipped out the windowsill,
catching herself a bird's-eye view
of sage-clad hills and famished bungalows.

Timid

For a moment
everything was still.
No barriers
or extraneous interruptions.

Peace

A northern mockingbird started to sing
and so did the satin's immortality,
only to be brushed away
by an angry burst of city air.

Fatal

WAVERING

He used to wake up before the sunrise
to write poems about our intrepid love affair.

Now he sleeps in till ten
and writes about other faces.
Offering exchanges like,

"Yeah, you just never seem to pop up in the pages anymore."

Coughing up the naked truth so effortlessly.

"Yeah, I thought so."

PRISCILLA

I locked eyes with her yesterday
as I held his unsteady hand.

My eyes are the only witness!

of this trivial convergence,
yet it feels like a bomb has burgeoned
onto my heartbeat.

Take another step!

I tell myself.

The world has not turned on you yet.

A CELESTIAL DEPARTURE

He often said,
"I dreamed of a life like this."

But once his eyes
refused to stargaze any longer,
the only life that persisted
left a bitter aftertaste
in his mouth.

As I spoon-fed him my feelings
as a remedy to his acrimony,
he spit up shards of apathy in return.
Leaving me soaked
in the drippings of his dissatisfaction.

KALOPSIA

How can I find security
in the one
who has grown accustomed
to leading a life
of looking the other way?

I want to feel protected,
taken care of,
yet I constantly feel abandoned,
looking for that Prince Charming to save me
when he's simply stuck in his own world.

When will I stop overdosing on the delusion
that life is still as colorful as it once was?

BOYS TOWN BLUES

I hide the unbridled truth from my friends
that our union is dancing on trembling strings.
I leave out the barbed wire growing on each note
and sing only the harmonies,
allowing the song to still be palatable for every ear.

I want us to be better.
I need them to want the same.

If I'm vomiting up your inadequacy
I want them to hold my hair back
and remind me that every note you sing
is bleeding shards of gold.
Even though that's a fallacy
I built onto your name.

But I've never made it this far with someone.
The odds of what we have on our side of town are 1 in 1,000,000.
And I don't want you to notice the 999,999 others waiting in line for you.

I'd rather be satisfactorily content with you
then irrevocably depressed without you.
I suppose I'll do what I'm best at,
hide behind the music.
Nobody shall ever know
how you shatter my song
every single day.

This is the best I'll get.

THE BOY WHO CRIED WOLF

A wolf in sheep's clothing.
You made your remarks
with a sly backhanded comment
slipped right under them.

You told me how I felt,
you never asked.
You decided what was best for us
without filling me in on the game plan.
Leaving me high and dry
with nobody but myself
to pick up my shattered heart of glass
you so playfully smashed onto the bedroom floor.

I cried out to you
with shards of your duplicity
sticking out of my soul.

You analyzed my wounds
and proceeded to tell me,

*"I can see that you're hurting,
but I'm not, and I don't know
what you expect me to do about that."*

THE LAST SUPPER

I gave you all my chips
because you called yourself the losing game.
But as I turned around
you sold every color
to the closest devil
who was willing to pawn you.

I've learned nothing good comes from
a docile disciple
and a justifying Judas
breaking bread together.

DEVIL'S ADVOCATE

Keep your friends close
and your enemies closer...

Look at me fondly, Lucifer,
Do not betray me!
Because I am on your side.

As far as you can see,
from all the way down there . . .

CANOROUS

You played musical chairs,
jumping in and out of my life.
Heartstrings pulled back and forth
like a tantalizing harp
as you patiently anticipated
the sound of the timer going off,
just so you could leave
an empty seat at my table,
yet again.

HORS D'OEUVRES

Tonight, I passed my voice around
to anyone who'd lend an ear.
God knows it's not you any longer!
Listening in love is a harmless act
but for you,
Jesus, it must be too much to bear!

A HABIT OF DESOLATION

I caught myself
wanting the suffering
to never subside.

I was yearning for
the melancholic taste
of his leftover coffee
and even hoping
for the lingering scent
of her indigo perfume
on my guitar strings.

I found comfort
in the solace of
turning back the clock.
In every sense,
and through every sense I could muster.

THE CHERRIES ON 14TH STREET

I knew I'd lost you
the moment you glazed over my eyes
like you didn't recognize them any longer.
I'd been concealing my needs
with metal bumpers
for too many nights;
when at last
I asked
and I pleaded
for a lasting moment,
you shut off our light and went to bed.

I marched outside to finish
the latter half of my cigarette
under the cherry tree.
But as I smoked you out of my system,
the lady next door screamed profanities at me,
saying I was blowing death into her window.
Maybe I was.
I stomped on my spirit
and counted each step back
to our bloodstained door.

As I grabbed the brass handle
and peered down the hallway,
I didn't recognize our house any longer.

GOING, GOING, GONE

He looks at me with disdain.

His skin can hardly keep his heart inside his chest any longer.

"Any longer?"

I ask him.
He doesn't respond.
He's gone.

"He's gone?"

He's already gone.

SELF-REFLECTING

Maybe it's me.

You left my hand unattended
for the last time
and pulled back the curtain
on our ambivalent fantasy.
You said it was time
we went our separate ways,
scratched off the scorecard
and put this love in a little box under our beds.
You threw me out of your life
like a ragged jacket donated to the local Goodwill.

Time for a new owner to claim my baggage!

Well, I'm still holding on
tighter than ever.

But I'm starting to realize
the figure I'm clinging to
is solely a ghost now.

Maybe it's me.

Because after all this passion
this anguish,
this mania,
this lust,
this avoidance,
this childish whimpering on my bathroom floor,

I'm so far from ready
to say goodbye to you.

Maybe I'm the toxic one.

HOLLYWOOD HANGOVER

Dry January
has been drenched in disarray
for the boy who is set on a journey
of self-discovery.

The adventure is one of loneliness
accompanied by a singular ice cube
lubricated with Maker's Mark,
striking my pain with temporary relief,
only to wake up in a sweat of sufferance
demanding its turn to speak.

MISTRIAL

My heart is perplexed on how to let you go
because the jury is still out on who you are.

Were you the unassuming saint
that all probabilities and coincidences worked out in your favor?

Or were you the nuanced and manipulative partner
who painted their red flags yellow?

Do I loathe you or do I mourn you?

Do I let go of the things that broke me and blame myself instead?

Or shall I hold tight to the scars and mark them

PROPERTY OF YOU.

Should I despise you or just continue hating myself?

1-800-MAKE-IT-WORK

Last night I got a call
from a New York area code.

I hoped it was your new line,
surprising me with an intention
of catching up,
spilling life stories
over a cup of cinnamon coffee.

Last night I got a call
from a New York area code.

It was a love hotline,
trying to sell me on
a virtual seminar called "How to get the guy back!"

Last night I answered a call
from a New York area code
and I hung up.

LOVING FOR SPORT

I don't know why I look at exes
like old scars
left on my shins
from summers past,
like tallies on a game card.

Even when I'm in love
I'm always wondering...
When is this jig up?
So I can call it a draw
and add them to my wall
of past trophies,
fragmented and stained
for the onlookers to come and see;
offering me sympathy as admission payment.

APPLES AND ORANGES

I clung to his essence harder
than I ever embraced hers,
yet my soul still shattered
in the cradle of their grasp
with every finger pointed at me.

As I wipe the familiar guilt
off my cheeks
my spirit lingers at the crossroads
of dawn and dusk.

I long for her whisper in the wind
and I crave his shadow from the sun
but neither of them
are waiting at the traffic light with me
intertwining fingers
through the unraveling of this enigma.

REDUCE, REUSE, RECYCLE

I regret you every Sunday night.
The evenings I wrote sonnets
proclaiming my love,
ones you left on the bedside table
to become a paper coaster
for your boiled water
to soak up
instead of sponging your heart
with the love
I so desperately
wanted you to accept.

At least we didn't waste any more paper.
You would've hated that.

TO-DO LIST #14

- Change my car oil
- Get hemp milk
- Sleep with somebody else
- Take my jacket to the dry cleaners
- Clean out the spam folder of my inbox
- Stop buying those cigarettes he loved to smoke
- Listen to "This Is What It Feels Like" without my stomach churning in concentric circles
- Let the ghost of him leave the foot of my bed

ECHOES IN THE PARK

He said I was right,
"You do have nervous palms,"
as he pinched the dimples
in my lower back,
pushing me up the stairs
to his one-bedroom fantasy.

He showed me the desk he built.
The paintings he bought.
And the dog he loved.
"This could be yours too."

It was like a reverie.
Every moment felt real.
Every moment felt new.
It was like his hands soaked the fear right out of mine.
Enchanting all my walls
to come crashing down
just for him.

But when the sun arose
over the abandoned park
that we danced in the night before,
I woke up alone.

I searched for the cabinetmaking mystic
that read my palms to capitulation
but all I could find was two indents
in the lower end of his mattress.
And the only echo I could hear now

was one of the neighbors
carrying a new coffee table
onto their porch.
Or maybe it was just a nightstand.

TO THE WIND

"A cautionary tale"
is what the canyons called him.
Carnations on a winter's day.
Charisma and greed wrapped up in an iridescent bow.
Enough secrets to pervade a landfill of his ex-lovers.
He dances with the devil as he hides from the September sun
that burns down onto his August atrocities.
That's why he owns curtains.

His eyes sing of truth
yet only his lips do the talking.
A doublespeak at times
that yells a chant of gold
in the afternoon heat
and whispers a hymn of deep violet
in the frigid morning hours.
But it will never catch up to him!

He can clean off his evening
with a dip in the sunken pool
filled with cold water dripping
from his canyon of tears.
Tears of every soul he's tangled his storm into.
Long before I came along.
And long after I'll leave.
How much longer can he go?
How far can the train travel
before it hits a stone wall of duplicity?
He'll say it's duplicity.
But the roses blooming

underneath his foundation
have been tended to for years
by his very own hands
and I keep cutting myself on the thorns.

Why have I never seen him bleed?

GROWING PAINS

I wonder if you're having these talks too.

With your mom,
your brother,
your best friend.

Comparing unfamiliar hands
with the indented memory of mine.

Putting the chemistry of lovers past
in a bullet-pointed lineup,

BEST TO WORST.

Wondering if that innate feeling of infatuation
will ever be found again...

Or,
if each time
you meet someone new
and fall for them
the feeling loses its intensity.

INSIDE

As I look around
the dreary walls of my mind,
I pull back the cobweb-stained curtains
to reveal a phrase
I penned to myself in chalk:

"You are not enough."

How sweet!

I grab a bucket of water
and start to scrub
the paint of worthlessness
off my subconscious.

THE STREET ARTIST

Your hair tousles
in the alleyway breeze
as you fold your head
into your hands,
hiding from the consequences
of your reality.

Draw me another picture of hope
and use it as a trope
to fill in the empty spots of love
you are incapable of giving anywhere.

Where,
where?

Show me where.

Where are you giving me your
"authentic truth,"
when the only conclusion you can come to
is an unfinished one
that leaves all parties involved
empty-handed,
crumpling up
scribbled sketches
on manila paper
as evidence
of why you fall short.

Shortsighted

I must be
to fall for the face
that folded first.

I am dumbfounded
at my instinctual abilities.
No longer able to trust
myself
when I gave all that trust to
you.

You never even bothered to
RETURN TO SENDER.
You let it die with the collateral damage
of our inconclusive love story.

A story?
Is it even a story,
if the boy is too scared
to sing me to sleep?
He just creeps back to his alleyway
to lay his head in his hands
as his hair tousles in the wind,
waiting for his next victim
to cross his path of locks.

COVETOUS

Sleeping with pencils under my pillowcase,
trying to squeeze as much clarity
out of your memory
and turn it into
some capitalist payoff
that will help my mother sleep better at night.

Because that's what artists do, right?
But will I ever succeed
when the life you've painted
has become the cryptic thief
of my joy?
I'm dripping ounces of sweet nothing onto your loose leaf.

CRUEL INTENTIONS

I lied to you
with a subtle kiss to your cheek.

You offered me
a broken promise,
one you could never follow through.

But it was for the story, right?

I loved her
and I loved you
but not me.
Never me.

Why do I always find myself here?

I lose everyone
that falls into my lap
because no one
can sustain loving a person
who has no strength in themselves.

THE MAN IN BLUE

You bought new bedsheets
to distract from the fact
that we haven't spoken in six weeks.
Periwinkle or some adolescent shade of blue.
Washing away the smell of me
with every wrinkled thread count.

Now my heart is good for nothing.
Except for a fickle memory
hiding in the cedar-lined walls
of your loudmouthed home.
You can still hear my heart beating in the rafters.
I'm sure you'd call the noise ~~of it~~ of me
"a drunken mistake."

JOURNAL ENTRY #298

I long for a reality where we could put a Band-Aid on our broken
hearts and call it a day.

I'm learning that one of the most important organs in our body
requires far more intensive care then we may have to offer, let alone
actively give.

We can't just patch up our feelings and forget about them,
they refuse to leave us until we truly deal with them.

So, how do we deal with it?

I'm still trying to answer that question myself.

The only foolproof step I've found
is that learning to listen to that microscopic voice inside
is where to begin.
Listening to the instinctual, calm, sincere person
hiding deep in your subconscious
is where serenity starts.

Pay attention to when your intuition calls out to you and asks to make
a necessary change.

Don't dismiss the red flags that the heart waves right in front of your
face.

COUPLES SHOWER

I sit crisscrossed
on cracked porcelain
as the rainstorm pours onto my lower neck.

I count each tile on the shower wall
for days that were beautiful with you.

As I reach number 97,
your old shampoo glimmers from the corner of my eye.
I pick it up and examine the ingredients
I used to massage into your hair.
The act of doing so was mundane,
but maybe *moments like that* were where our love lived?

As I wipe the dust off your Head & Shoulders,
I let it take my place in the torrential downpour from above.

I give myself the courage to stand up on my own two feet
and stare at the fogged glass
that's sweating itself into new levels of haze and obscurity,
the glass where we used to write our initials and a cupid's heart to go
with it.

I'd draw the letters.
You'd sketch the arrow.
A perishable emblem of our love.

The sketches of us are long gone now,
but I can't help my hand from falling into old habits.

As I engrave our names into the fog
I can feel your hand guiding mine,
each curve and curlicue carved with intention.
But at the very end,
you fall short.
My eyes refocus to see
two halves of a broken heart in the smoky reflection.

We were nothing more than a game of overstepping and falling short.
No "*two initials*" could carry the weight of a fractured organism
through the new year.

Why did I put it all onto you?
Why did I give you everything
when you never asked for it?
Why did I anoint the broken boy
to validate the most vulnerable parts of myself?
Why did I demand everything grandeur
when your love lived in the prosaic?

I listen closely to the beats of my heart without you.

One.
Two.   Three.
Four.   Five.   Six.
Seven.   Eight.   Nine.   Ten.

I count each hum
and shake my wrists in the water
that used to flush your ruby cheeks with renewal.
I wait for some magical vibration to shock my body

into waking up from this nightmare.

I turn the dial hotter,
but the steam offers no relief.

The only constant
is the drum that dances against my rib cage.

Our love was inverse.

You never could love me like I wanted you to.

And that's not your fault.

UNTYING LOOSE ENDS

I looked into his weary eyes
then down at the scarlet string
that once tied our hearts
into a kaleidoscope of ecstasy.
It was now shriveled and spotted,
scaling each of our bodies for any life source,
taking years off our happiness
with every woven inch.

Why am I still holding on?

I saw his face right in front of me
but I no longer saw *him*.
I'd roped his anatomy into a crimson contract
that was only active to substitute my very own absence of self-worth.

Why am I still holding on?

I took a deep breath
and began to tear the rope
right down the middle,
tears crystallizing as shards of scarlet
bled onto my hands.
I kept tearing until his soul
faded into the void of yesterday.
And then

I woke up.

III

ANASTASIS

GOLDEN STATE

The brakes are singing
on the Five freeway.
Off-key, might I add!

California has a landscape
that keeps you enthralled
in the hills of possibility
during the mindless snarl-ups.

Count the broken palms
on the highway shoulders
and leave your fear of being
less than
right next to the shattered car glass.

Speed up
and leave your phone in the back seat.
It may be a lot of stop and go
but you're certain
you'd rather coast here
then jet in any other sky.

I'm wide-awake now,
it's morning.

ABSCISSION

The violet orchid
falls onto my floor.
The volatile lover
falls on his luck

yet again.

Both lost hold of their foundation,
both cut off,
looking for resurgence.
When will the sun let them bloom again?

PROSAIC PROFESSIONS

It's been twelve months.
The hummingbirds still fly at sunrise.
The ice maker still makes a thunder sound
and the bagels down the block
still sell out by noon.
Even if the rest of the world
continues to go on,
I don't know if I can make it,
admiring the mundanities of life
without you by my side.

THE IRON CURTAIN

I loved you for the mystery,
the chase,
the avoidance,
the fascination of
"Will I ever truly know who you are?"
What goes on in your life
and will I ever actually be a part of it,
or am I just lucky enough
to witness it up close?

You were something like Olivia.

She was enigmatic,
alluring,
and always
on another plane of reality
I could simply never reach.

But damn, I always wanted to.

I thought you would let me in
like she eventually did,
but my erroneous hope
left me broken
in the process
of breaking down your walls.

THREAD COUNT

The chilled sun on a September morning
crept in through my crooked shades
as I adjusted your underwear
back onto my broken frame.

I reached for your skin
but only found an indent
from the body of a boy
who told me he would love me
but let his infidelity get in the way.

Of what he promised,
of what I promised,
of what we made.

A sacred vow,
vowing to love one another
till the bed of our passion broke
into a million thread counts.

I wish I could say
I knew it was coming
but I didn't know I'd be blindfolded
as he pulled the sheet out from underneath me.
Under where
he laid his heart of holes
to rest every night
after slowly poking dents in mine.
Your pillow was cold.
I smelled a lingering of tobacco

as I put my head down
and closed my eyes,
imagining the version of me
that once slept with rose quartz
under my pillow,
manifesting the boy
who gave me a feast of love
for the fervent moments of passion
that were going,
going,
gone.

Now leaving me with nothing
but his scraps to fill up on.

On to the next one I go.
Will he look like you?
No.
But maybe I'm just kidding myself.
As I tuck the pink stone back under my neck, yet again
I sing a soft hymn of the passion I once knew.

I turn back around and try to find your eyes
in the man lying next to me now,
hoping he doesn't notice
the indent of you
on the left side of my bed.

MAN ENOUGH

There is an intoxicating connotation attached to the word "man."

But why does the world seem to get drunk off one small word so easily?
How can so much importance and pressure
be squeezed into three letters?
Who gave indispensable meaning to the word "man"?

Was it Socrates?
Was it Abraham Lincoln?
Was it your Uncle Johnny
after he had six beers and shouted
he'd knock out that guy down the bar
if he looked at him sideways
one more time?

Whoever the author,
the comprehensive meaning of the word is
instilled in our world today.
Through biology,
throughout social constructs,
through interpersonal relationships,
and through how we see ourselves.

To be a man.

To be a man
is to provide.
To protect.
To compete.
To survive.

To prevail.

But how do we live up to that?
How do we fill the weight of those size 13 shoes?
How can we achieve the goal that our fathers set forth in front of us?

To be a man.

"Be watchful, be firm in the faith, act like men, be strong."

To be a man.

"Do you see the man skillful in his work? He will stand before kings; he will not stand before other obscure men."

To be a man.

"Likewise, fellow husbands, dwell with them according to knowledge, giving honor unto the wife, as they are the weaker vessel . . ."

To be a man.

"Iron sharpens iron, and one man sharpens another."

To be a man.

As I look up from my grandfather's King James Version
and into the mirror,
I see a face that's grown solemn.
Sunken cheeks
and bloodshot eyes,

clenching my fists,
hoping for any sense of certainty
in my manhood
to just
click.

But the only click I hear
is my shoes against the pavement.
Racing.
Chasing after a version of me that
has never existed.

I've sat in boardrooms,
locker rooms,
and bedrooms
praying that the other men
won't smell the stench of inauthenticity
spilling off me.

So, I wear cologne.
I keep up with football.
I eyeball stocks,
size up women,
and unwind in front of a video game screen
where I kill and kill and kill
until I don't feel the weight of man any longer.

When does this ideal of hedonistic masculinity
I've become addicted to
start to fulfill me?

When will this control I'm so desperately chasing
actually be accomplished?
It wasn't till I was doubled over on the bathroom floor,
crying into the arms of my mom,
begging God to make me straight,
that I realized the idea of "man" I've been prescribed
is not real.

The word "man" is not finite.
It's not limited.
It's complex.
It's elastic.

The critical qualities of man are based in duality.

Yes, I want to be resilient.
But I also want to be vulnerable.

I can be strong in the face of adversity
but I am not more righteous
than any woman or man that passes by my window.

I am leaving the idea of virility in the past
and starting to look for joy in every corner,
regardless of how small or weak it makes me look.

As my heart softens
over the cerulean scars
that have resulted from trying to be
"man enough,"

I take baby steps.
Not big manly steps.
But steps.
Towards the real version of me.
Walking towards the person I know I can be.
Singing a song of freedom,
free from the shackles of who I was supposed to be.

Letting that soul deep inside my bones
run free
and dance along the spectrum
of vibrant colors,
feelings
and impulses
that have been locked up inside my bones.

As I lose myself in the song of my truth,
I don't feel tight anymore.
I don't feel tense,
I don't feel restricted.
I don't feel pressure, to keep up the facade,
to be a man.

My masculinity cannot be scaled, weighed or dilated.

I am the only person who can define what being man enough is for me.

-1 Corinthians, 16:13, -Proverbs 22:29, -Proverbs 27:17, -1 Peter 3:7

PSILOCYBIN

Do you ever find yourself dreaming
about the night under the sparkling willows
somewhere off Topanga Canyon?

The night we said our vows,
our friends sat in a circle
and watched us profess
the love we felt so wholly
for one another
as tears fell onto their scarlet crowns.
The drugs were strong
but our passion overpowered any substance,
filling us with an iridescence so strong
I think we reached heaven.
Although we didn't sign a piece of paper
my soul felt betrothed to yours
from that magical evening on.

AURORA

I curl up in front of the fireplace
wearing your favorite sweatshirt,
thinking of the cavemen
and love-obsessed city folk
that came before me.

Why did our universe
beat up the wrong guy?

Why can't I wrap my head around
the treacherous loss of you?

Am I living life on Mars now?

Is that why you're so far away?

DEAD END

I'm looking for answers from a boy
who simply does not have them.

He isn't hiding the salacious truth
in his coat pocket
or building a moral high ground
over my ambivalence.

He is simply
emotionally underdeveloped.

He is not capable
of giving me the answers
I am so desperately searching for.

COUNTERCULTURE

Indifferent about his actions
and how ripe cherries
were perceived in the moonlight.
Erogenous anecdotes
offered in return for a prize
I was rotten I never received.
Knocking heads with the guy
who played a game I was allergic to.
His competence waged war with every fear of mine
and I spent my Sundays choking on stems,
trying to tie a knot that enticed him.

I longed for a Monday where brazenness
was a vitamin in the milk
I poured over my morning cereal.

I screamed to Jesus in the sky
and demanded confidence
in the name of comparison.
He never answered.

So, I got on the George Washington Bridge
and let my bottle of tiny blue pills
go swimming in the Hudson.

AUGUST

I peek through the window
of video clippings
from a Parisian summer,
reminiscing on the storyline
that led me there with you.

Striped shirts,
singing trumpets
and scraps for supper.

But as I look up from the Will
I just kissed in the same spot
where I cried to you last,
I feel wary
of what's to come.

Is this moving on?
Making peace with both scenarios.

Both likely,
both devastating.

INTROSPECTION

Searching for concrete answers
to the open-ended conclusions
written along the walls of my subconscious.
I reach out to my third eye for guidance
yet her phone line seems to be disconnected these days.

Instead of doing a house call,
I got her tattooed on my wrist.
Now she's stuck with me,
permanently aware,
watching over my highest self.

Please,
shed some insight, miss.

"WHY DID THIS HAPPEN TO ME?"

Those adolescent hands
still knock on the cracked wood
of my bedroom door,
crying for answers to a question
that was thrust upon me
long before I could ever comprehend
the gravity of what was being asked.

Though subjectivity may be out of the "question"
when the anguish that bellowed
from his teenage grasp
cracked the blood vessels in the nape of my neck.
Each finger he pressed into my chaste legs
shattered every shard of innocence
I had that frigid afternoon.
He said I was no longer a "boyish fool,"
I was a "man with experience and edge."
I told him I agreed with him,
as I picked up my Scholastic Book Fair bag
and ambled my feet all the way home.

When the February hailstorm came,
each birthday candle looked like
eight desolate pillars of my past.
I blew out every flame with my eyes wide open.
I took a bite of my pound cake
as the burden of yesterday
continued its journey down my throat.
I rubbed my stomach to settle
but the sprinkles of his cyclical ravishments

had already found their new home
in my bloodstream.

I've tried to clean them out,
throw them up
and burn off any memory left
of that ill-fated afternoon,
but the bitter taste has never left my tongue.

There is no cogent answer
that justifies the question
that eight-year-old boy
is spray-painting onto my bedroom door.
The only verbal remedy I can offer
is a rejection of his question.

SHADOW WORK

Dear Prudence,
I'm here to help you now,
tell me your troubles
and I'll pass you
the effervescent bandage of forgiveness.

Here Prudence,
walk with me
on the cobblestone streets
and listen to the sound of your shoes
making a mark amidst the darkness.

Listen Prudence,
nobody can hurt you here,
only your own mind,
so let it dance off into the boundless sky
and it will bother you no more.

Please Prudence,
come out to play
and I will show you
the unconditional love
you never received.

FOREST LAWN DRIVE

Sticking my head
out the car window,
letting my hair dance
in the September wind.

I'm on my way
to listen to the cicada
that sings swing music
outside my bedroom window
while I chew on shooting stars.

Tonight,
I'll drink my tea
and try to sit in this pain;
rewriting it into something beautiful.

EGO PLAY

I'm learning to live
with the pit in my stomach.
I'm learning to stomach
the fears,
the regrets,
the inadequacies,
that have blistered my point of view.

Nothing that stings will hurt forever.
Nothing that intoxicates me will keep me high indefinitely.

I'm learning to dance
in the ever-changing
continuum of life.

Nothing is finite.
Nothing about me is fixed.

I'm learning to love
the pit of passion
within my soul
that yearns for more
and whispers to it,
saying...

Right now, everything you are in this moment is enough.

BENEVOLENCE

Keep that paragraph in your notes app.
No contact speaks louder
than any five-sentence conjugation
of lukewarm nostalgia and broken hearts
ever could.

They're only special
because you named them so.
They're only idolized
because you saw your own love
showered onto them.

It's wonderful that you see
the beauty in everyone
but it's time
to start saving those efforts
for those who see the magnificence in you.

Start with yourself.

UPWARD AND ONWARD

I threw out your toothbrush this morning,
while spinning Carole King
for all my neighbors to hear.
She said *it's too late, baby!*
Though,
I do have to agree with her.
We really did try to make it.

SEARCHING FOR SOVEREIGNTY

Blackbird under the freeway pass,
seize my soul and take it to the skies!

Feed it to the cumulus clouds
and fill it up with the acid tears that beg to fall
on this sweltering Californian city.

Then return my essence,
a man renewed
with faith in myself,
so that I may never lose
the concept of autonomy.

IN THE TREES

So many temporary tenants
have it wrong
when it comes
to Los Angeles.

They write of
deceit,
hubris,
and
heartbreak
from the City of Stars . . .
but they were simply
searching for something
that was never here
to begin with.

Melt into the pot.
Don't burn a new plate
and say it's bleeding fruits and nuts.
Move with the breeze of the palm trees.
Don't break the gravel
and throw it against the wind.
Let me sing my song of love
to the City of Angels
in peace.

This is where
I always long
to belong.

SEEDS OF MY SOUL

A year ago today,
I was a shell of a human being.

Spilling out harsh truths and broken fears
to anyone who'd lend an ear.

Looking in the mirror now,
I see a man
who has outgrown
exposing wounds,
waiting for someone else
to apply the Band-Aid.

Today,
I offer myself
a shield of solace
as I continue to endure more change
than I ever deemed myself
capable of.

The new me is just around the corner,
but he's always been a part of me,
he's just sprouting.

EPICENE

Oh, how it feels
to sing a song of blue jays
then do the dance with a rose finch!
Double stepping between each beat,
"Never making up his mind,"
they whisper under my shoes
as they tap
onto the linoleum floor.
I make snow angels in his linen
and paint Madonnas in her cheeks.
Why must I choose?
When my tried and true
is as simple as
bleeding violet kisses
onto any soul
that merely connects with mine.

JOURNAL ENTRY #305

Coca-Cola in Joan's favorite green bottle.
Childhood photos taped onto the bathroom mirror.
Allman Brothers immortalizing themselves on top of my vinyl mat.
Walking from 76th Street to 14th with their hand intertwined in mine.
Heart-shaped necklaces with an arrow running through the center.
Eucalyptus from the market under my showerhead.
Feet under the covers on a November night.
Fool's gold under my pillow for good luck.
Bagels and coffee with my best friend on Sunday.
California rain on the February windowsill.
The lush greenery of Griffith Park after said rain-shower.
Christmas lights strung along the balcony in June.
Hand-rolled cigarettes at the outdoor bar with an old friend.
That one bookstore in La Cañada.
Eight p.m. in the heat of July.
Dodging traffic and taking Nichols Canyon with the windows down.
The Lovers II by René Magritte.
Perpetual kissing at the front door when I'm already running late.
The scent of their perfume lingering on my university sweatshirt.

I spent most days
chasing this kind of heaven.

WHAT I WOULD'VE DONE DIFFERENTLY

In retrospect,
healthy love
is sitting with that person
in all of their pain.
Not trying to overanalyze it,
speed through the process
or fix anything.
But simply lying next to it
with a tender hand.

BASIL STREET

As I gaze into
the pink house
with the blue stained shutters,
I reminisce on your cherry cheeks
and how they may never grace my eyes again.

"And that's alright,"
I tell myself.

Because I know the memory will never leave me.

Just like the love I have for myself.

A type of love
you could never give me.

NEW YEAR'S DAY

The inner conversation
of broken regrets
and fears of yesterday
needed to be had
so that I could hang up
that emotional baggage
and let it dry out
of my subconscious,
filling that space
with a bouquet of lilies.

There are sunny afternoons ahead.

DECORUM

Twirling around in the microwave reflection.
Fitzgerald reverberates off the plaster
while trumpets and loose strings
fill the amphitheater of my uneasy mind.

I know how to meet a day of
confusion and complication
and offer it an evening of
certainty and simplicity.
The tools are right there.
I just have to implement them.

Tonight,
I will.

Play the song a tad louder please!

ACKNOWLEDGMENTS

A massive thank you to Michelle Halket, Beau Avery Adler, Molly Ringle, and everyone at Central Avenue. You guys are my life raft. Thank you for helping me tell my story with such enthusiasm and compassion.

Thank you to the entire team at Simon & Schuster.

Thank you to my superstar manager Jered Servello / everyone at Stride for supporting me (and not laughing in my face when I said I was writing a collection of poetry).

Thank you to Abraham for being my guardian angel; this book wouldn't be here without you.

Thank you to Grace for believing in me when I had no idea how to do it myself. Your endless inspiration, help, and encouragement were the bedrock upon which this book was built.

Thank you to Mom and Dad for learning how to understand me and not discouraging my creativity.

Thank you to Brielle for being there through every read through, every cover, every uncertainty of this book (and life). You are my rock.

Thank you to Logan for being my fearless liaison. You helped craft the first pitch of this book in September 2020 and countless versions since. For that and so much more, I am forever grateful.

Thank you to Emma for always championing my writing, even when I felt small.

Thank you to Alyssa for being the unwritten prologue to my book. You feed my soul.

Thank you to Megan for assuming the position as big sister and carrying me through life (in and outside of Stars Hollow).

Thank you to Karan for being my brother on this journey. I am proud to be a man because of you. I'll see you for bagels and coffee at noon.

Lastly, thank you to every person (there are more than two) who inspired the words in this book. Thank you for the joy and thank you for the pain. You are living proof that I can love a person so deeply. I will do my best to turn that love inward for every day that's to come. Have fun figuring out which ones are about you.

Christian Weissmann is a writer and actor, born and raised in the suburbs of Chicago. His writing has appeared in the *Los Angeles Times* and *Huffington Post*. He's been on shows such as *Saved by the Bell*, *Dear White People*, and *American Housewife*. Weissmann has sought to pursue a life of vulnerability, personified through all creative mediums. *Her, Him & I* is his debut poetry collection.

"DO I CONTRADICT MYSELF?
VERY WELL THEN,
I CONTRADICT MYSELF.
I AM LARGE.
I CONTAIN MULTITUDES."

—WALT WHITMAN